When I Grow Up

A Free to be Me 😊 Book

STACY PRICE, PhD

Fulton Books
Meadville, PA

Published by Fulton Books 2022

ISBN 979-8-88505-223-8 (paperback)
ISBN 979-8-88505-225-2 (hardcover)
ISBN 979-8-88505-224-5 (digital)

Printed in the United States of America

To my mom, who put us first,
Who was proud of herself.
But who loved being a mom the most.

One day I sat in class.
I was very proud.

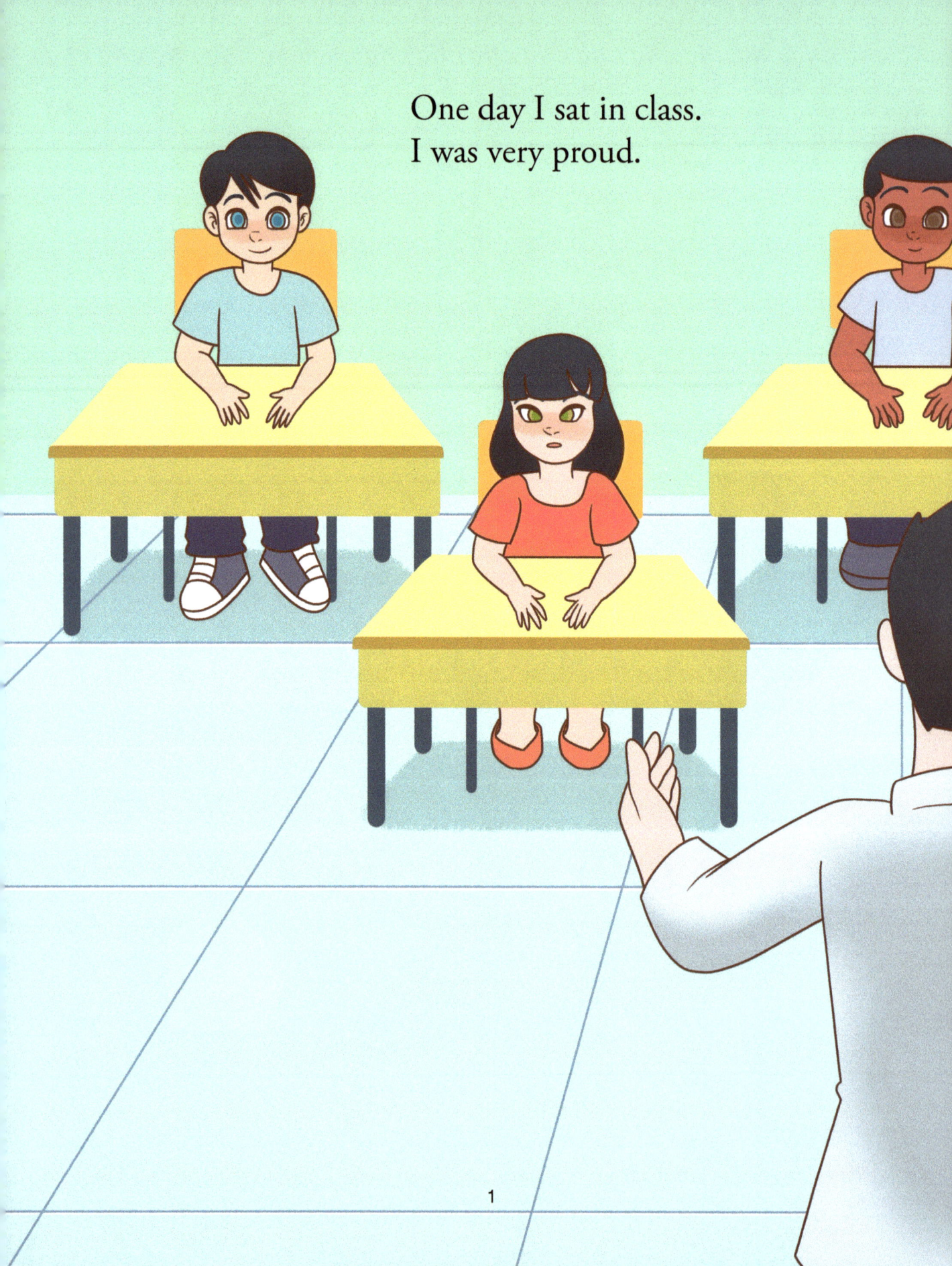

I wanted to raise my hand,
And I wanted to shout so loud!

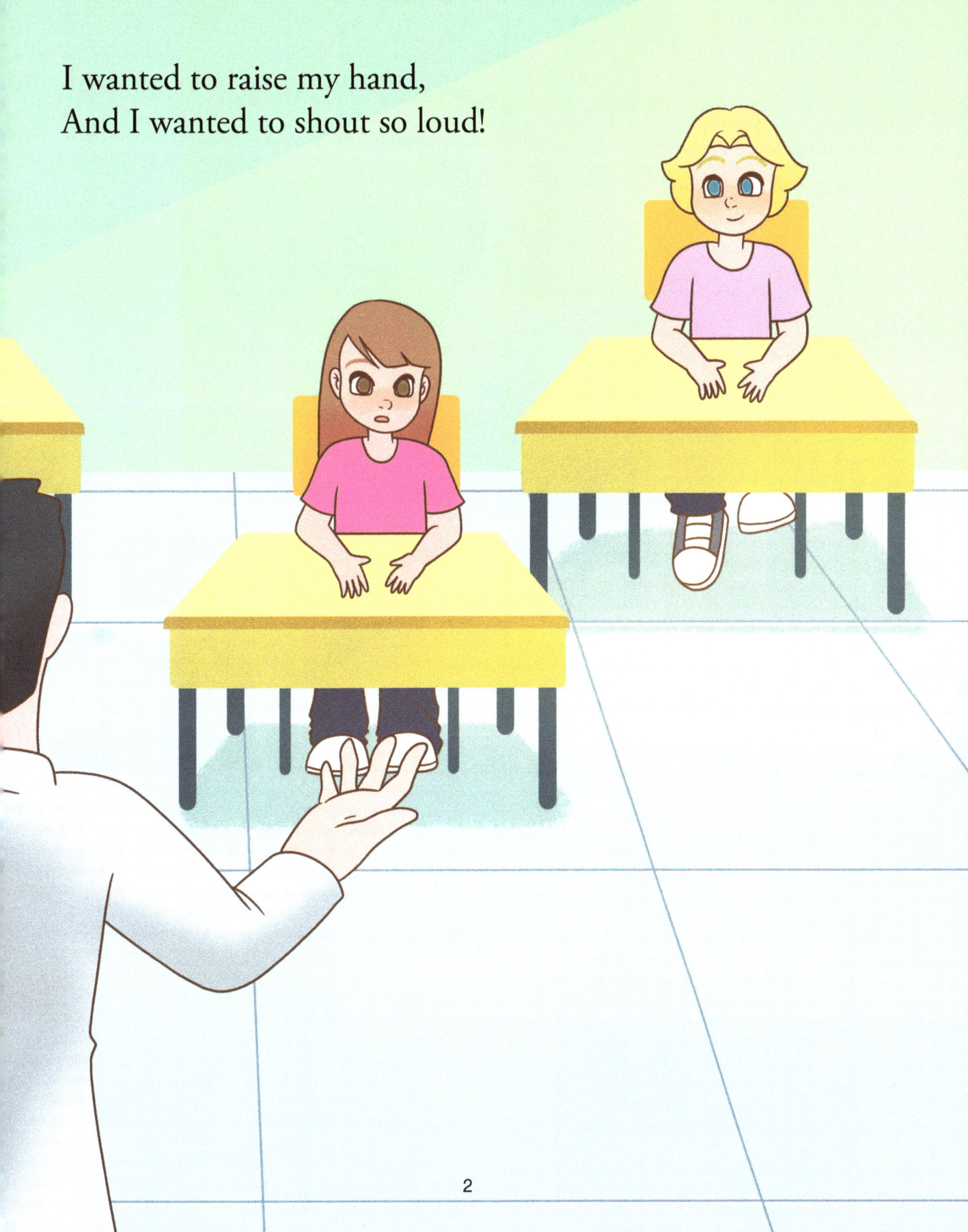

The teacher asked us what we wanted to be
When we are big like him.

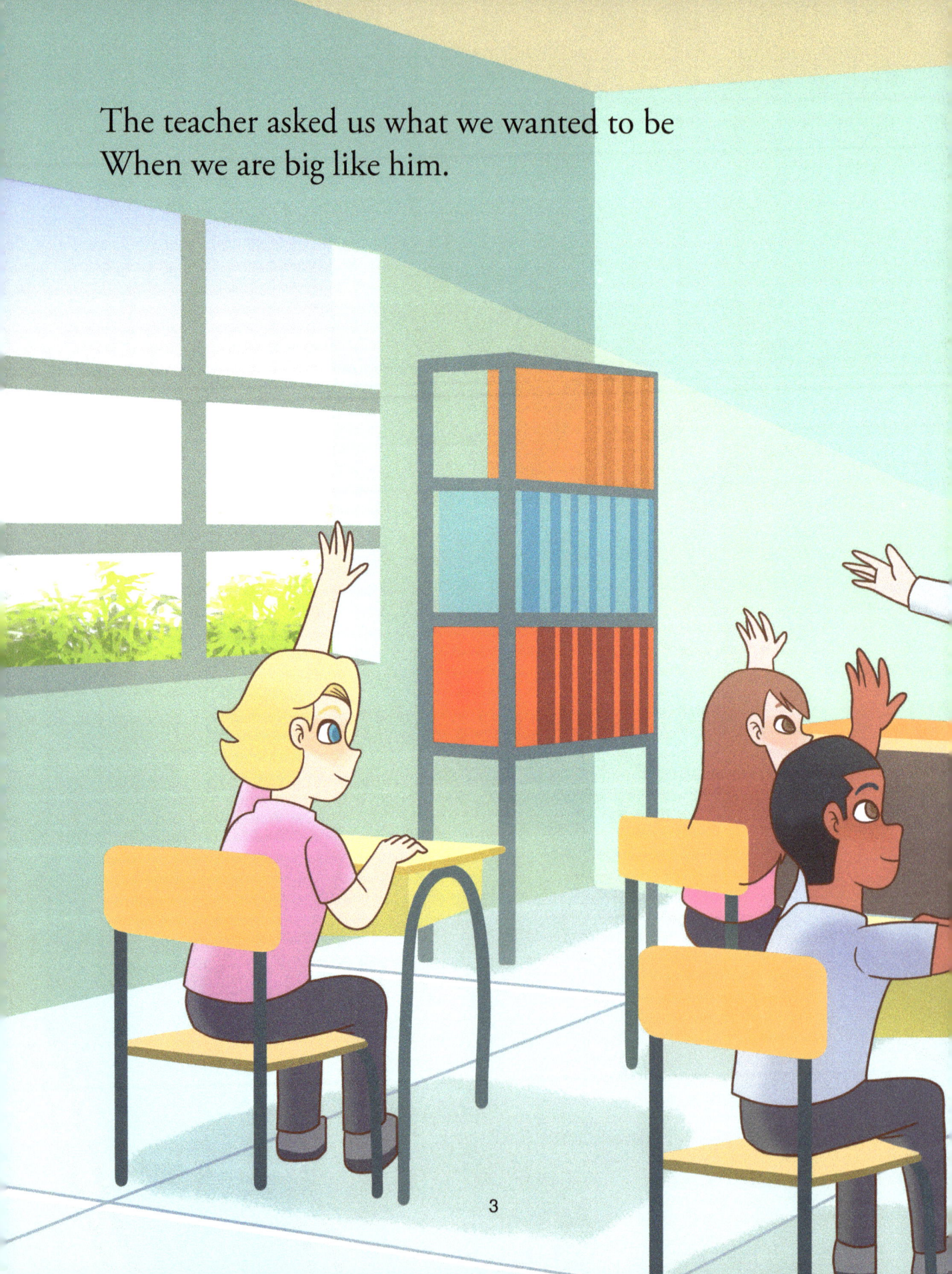

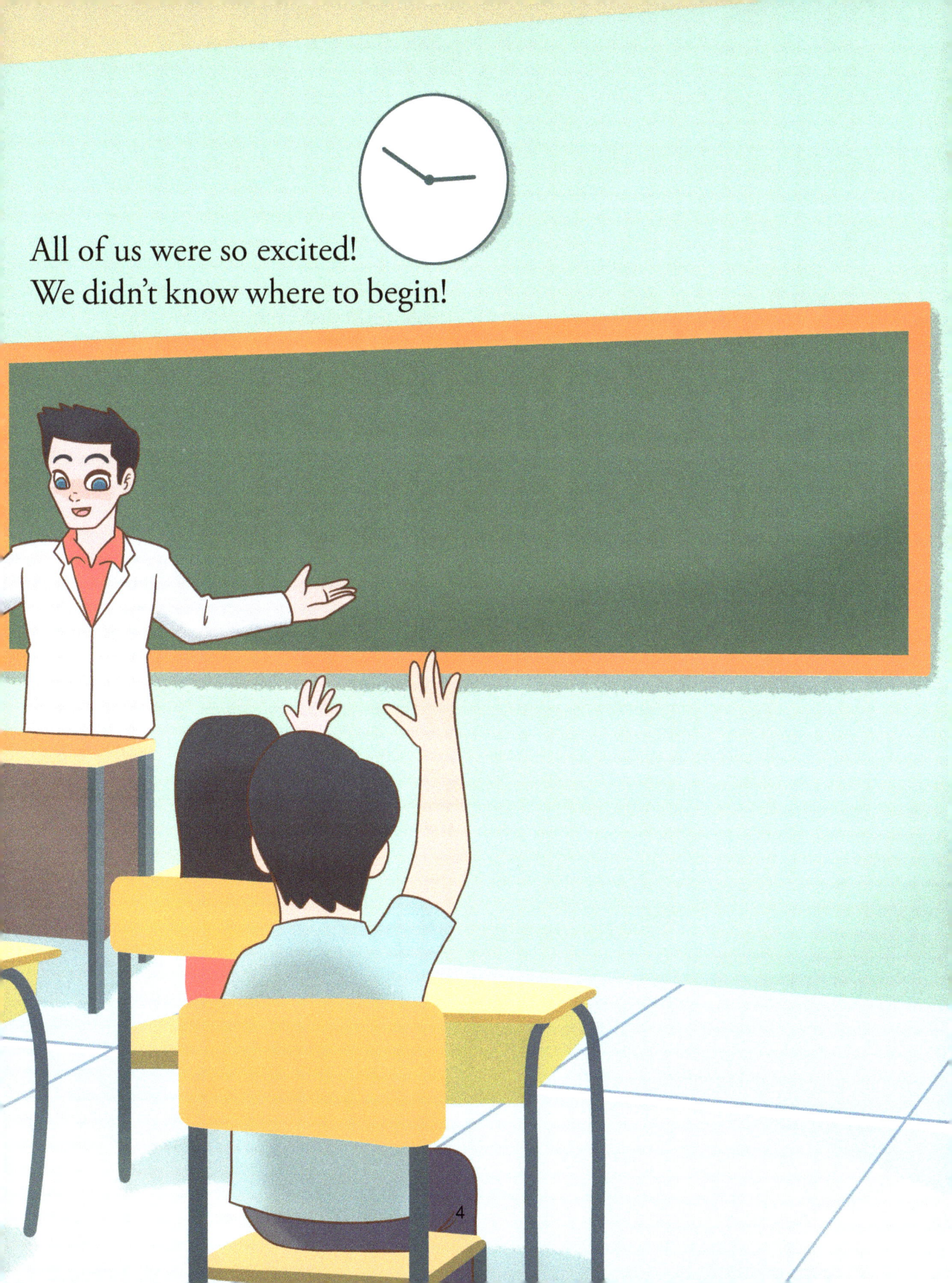

All of us were so excited!
We didn't know where to begin!

One friend said they wanted to be a doctor.
One other said they wanted to be a teacher.

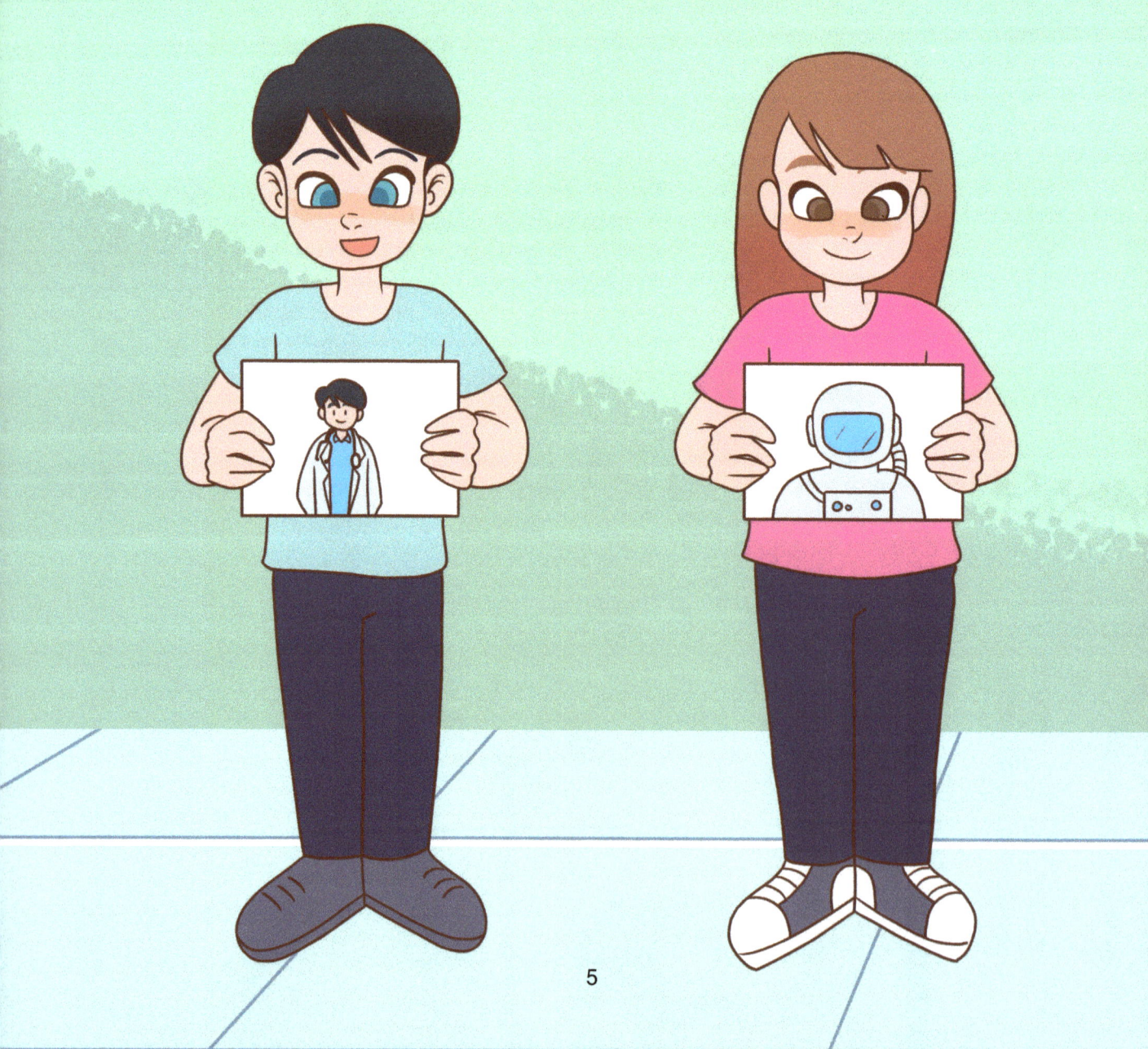

Someone else said an astronaut,
And my best friend said a preacher.

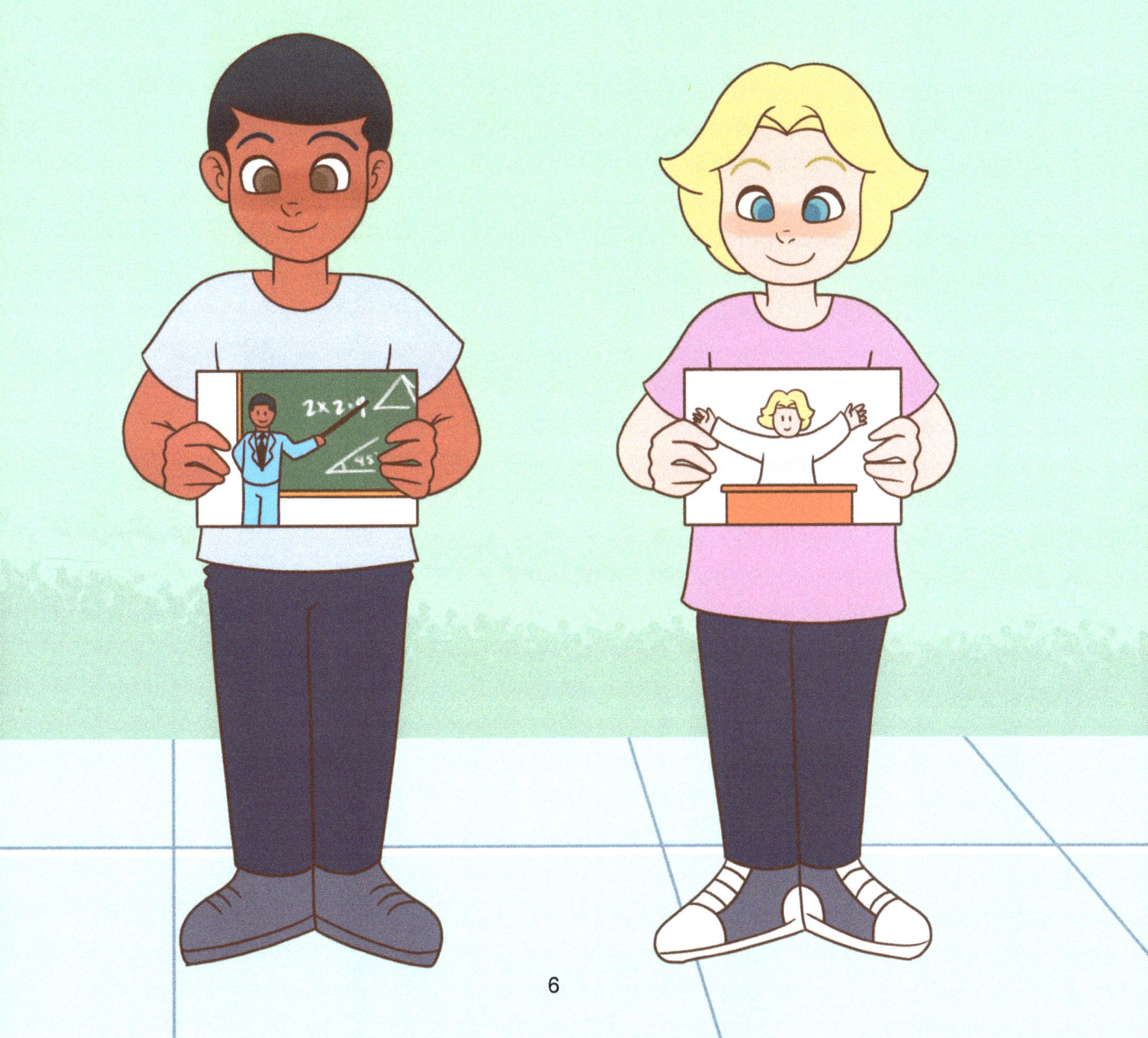

Suddenly, the teacher said my name.
I was so happy to be called on!

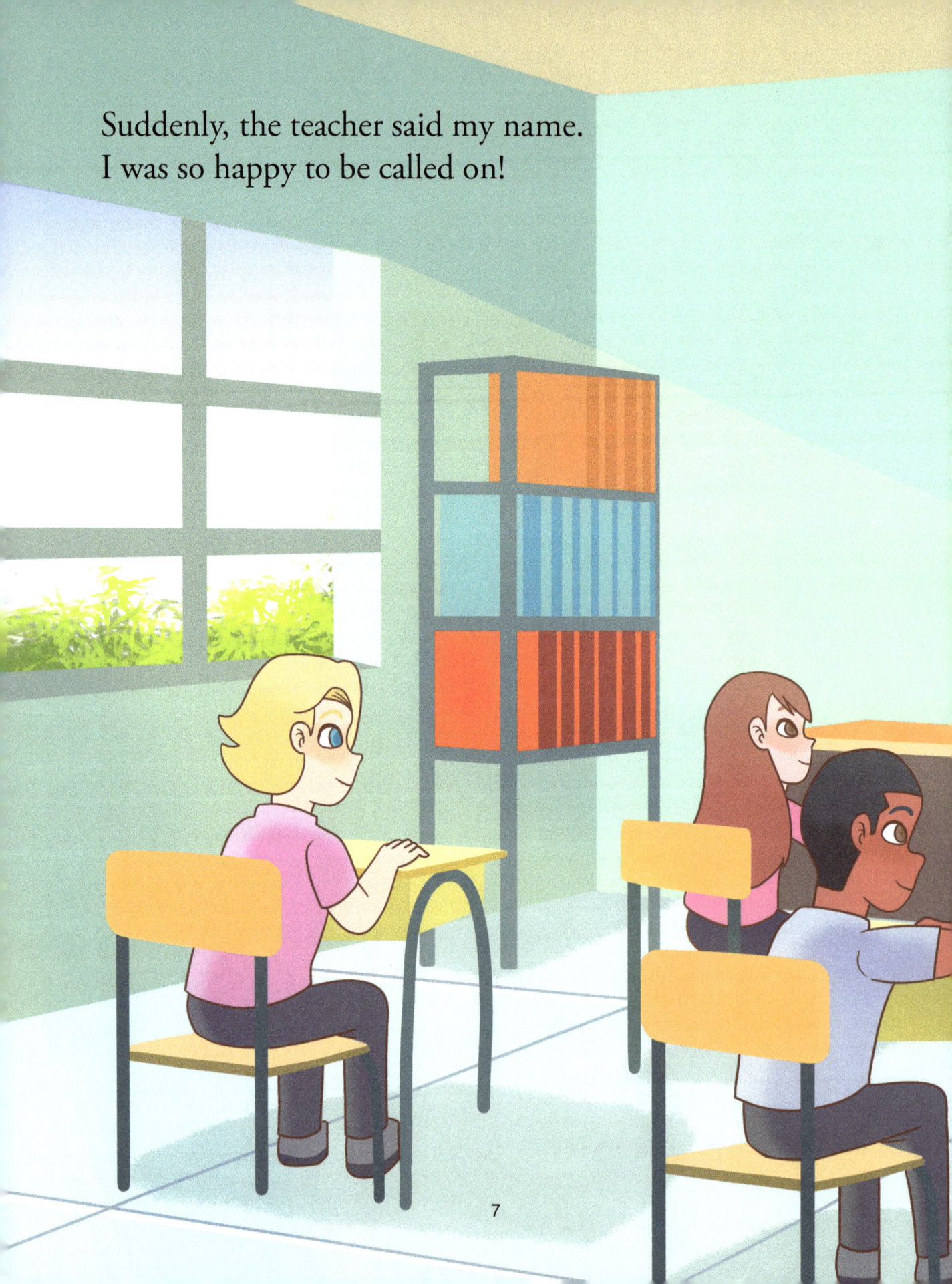

I stood up and said, "When I grow up,
I want to be a mom!"

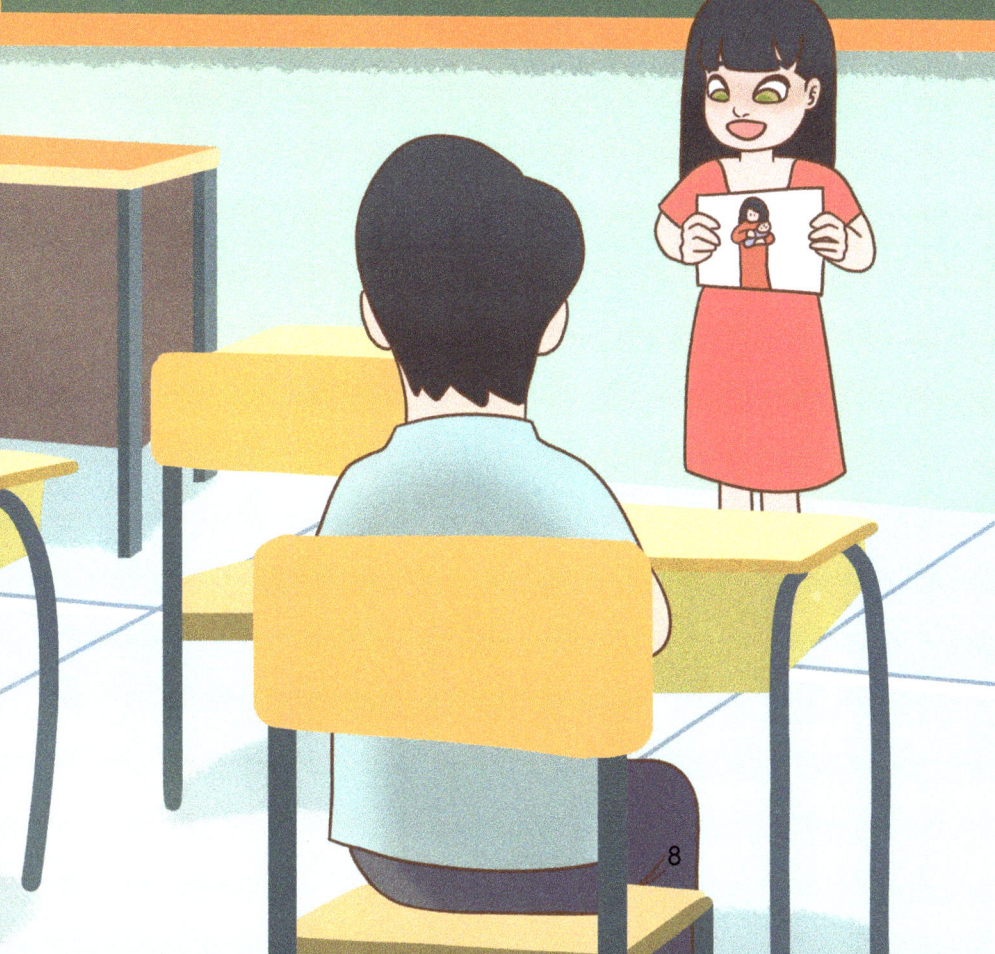

8

Everyone was laughing,
And it made me very sad.

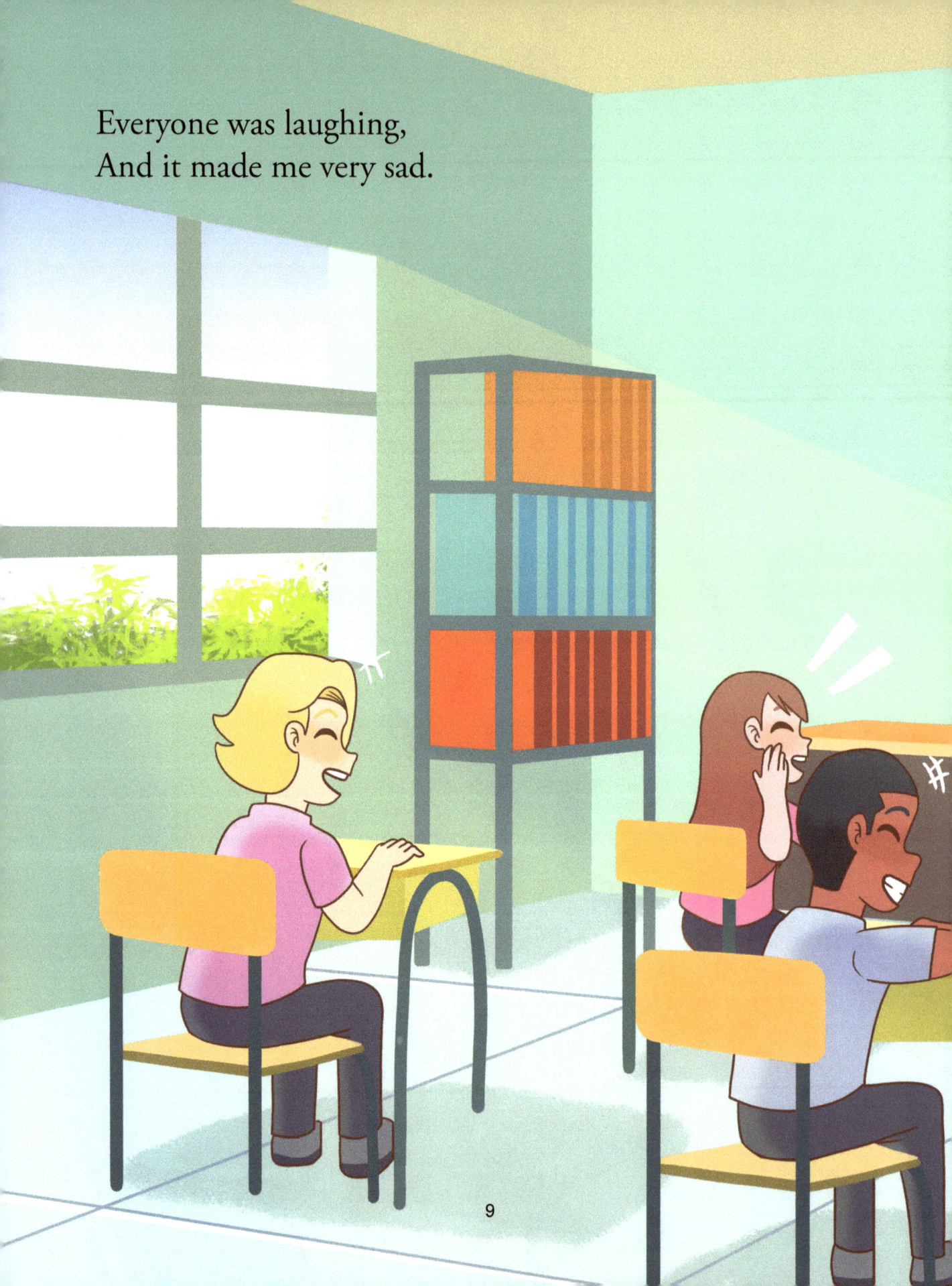

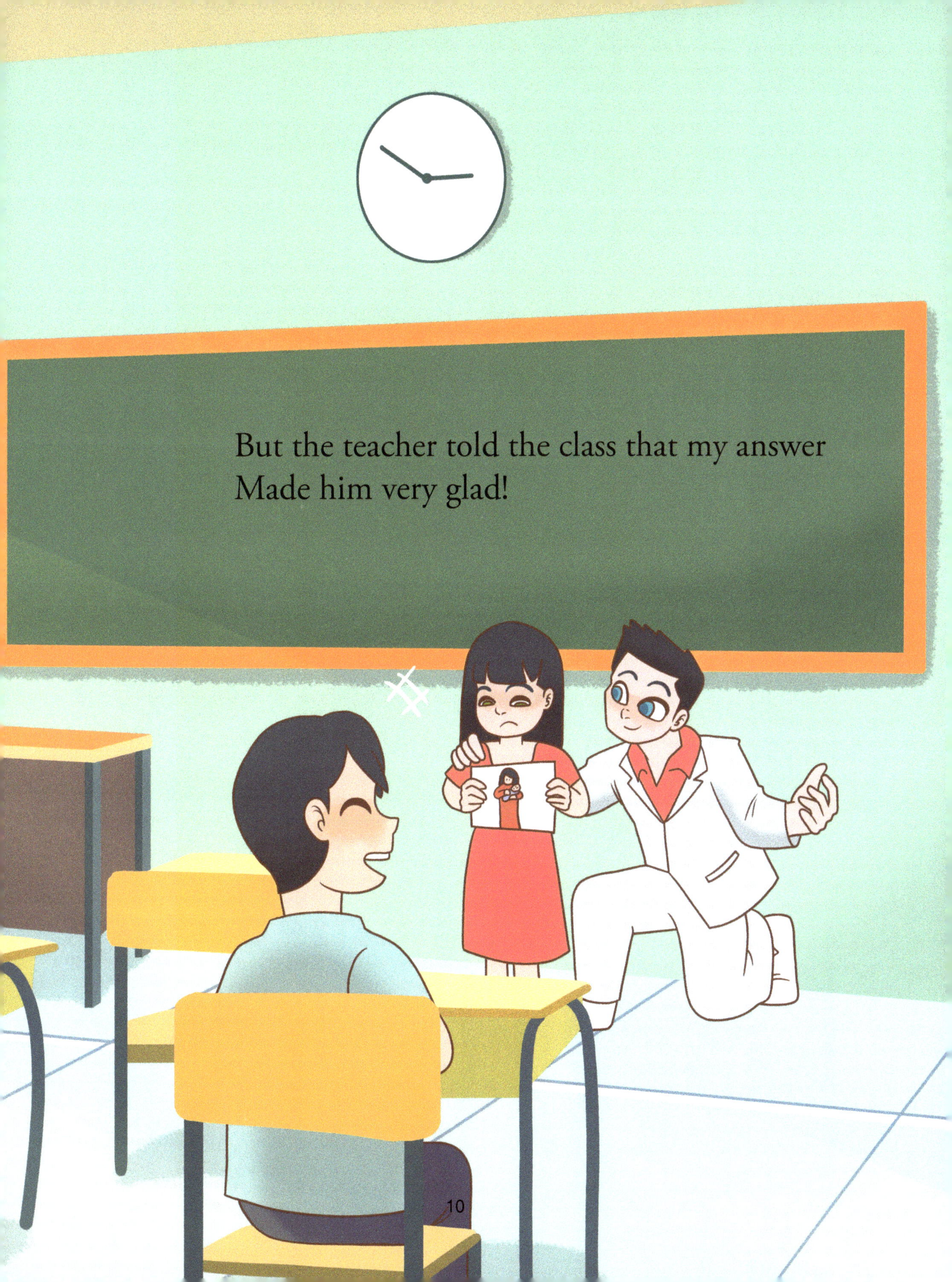

But the teacher told the class that my answer
Made him very glad!

He said, "Being a mommy is so important!
The job of parents is very big!

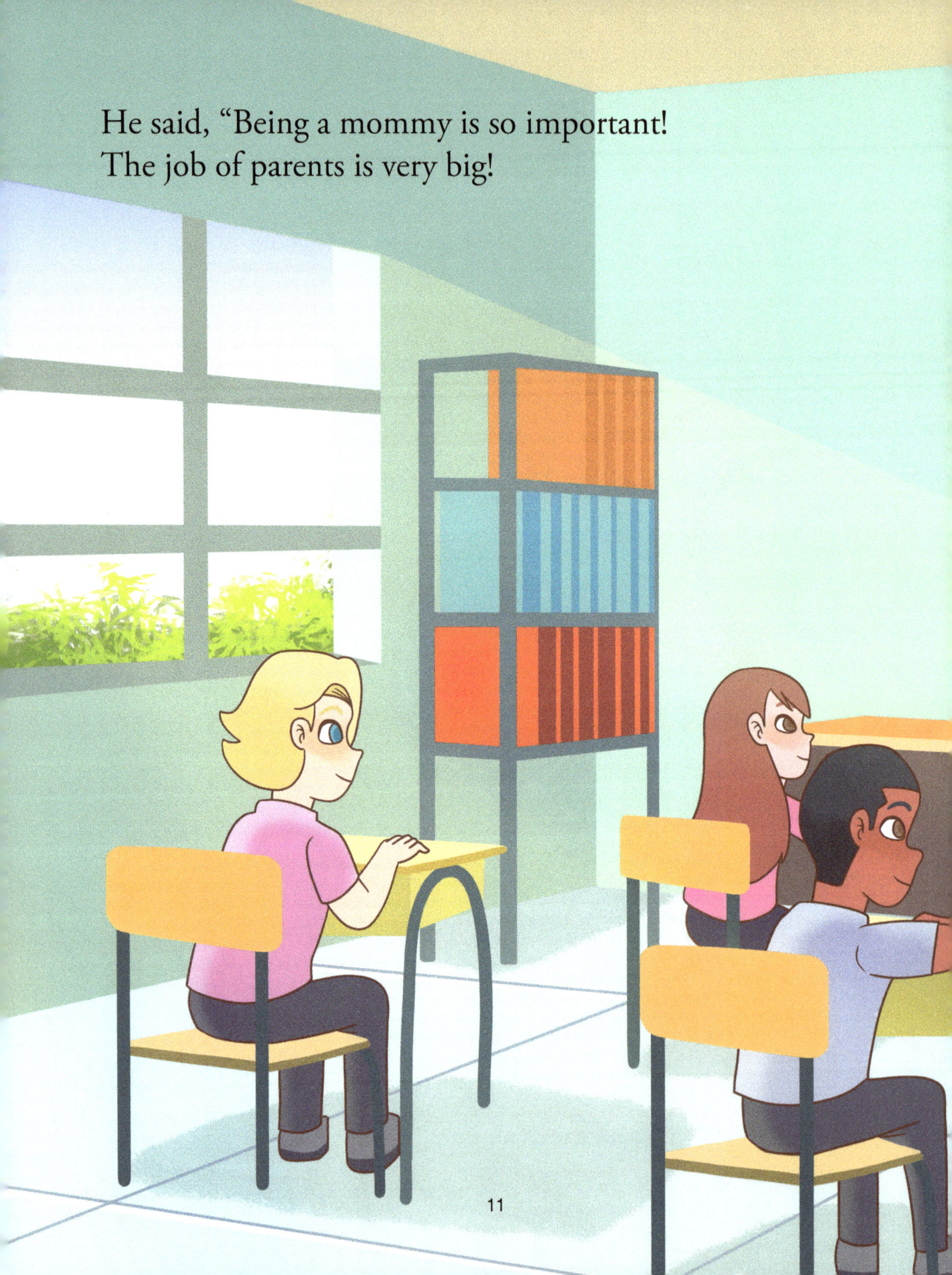

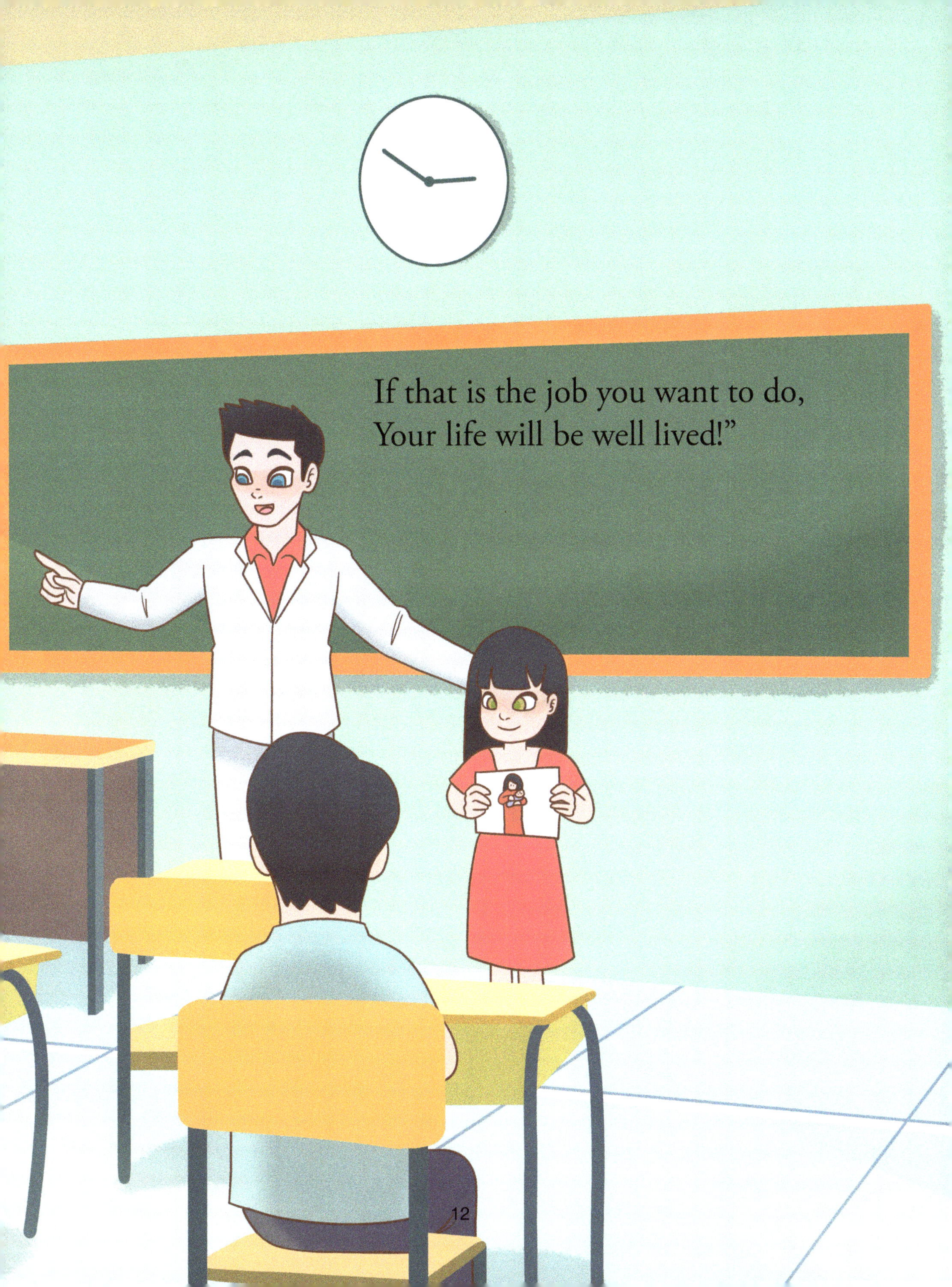

If that is the job you want to do,
Your life will be well lived!"

12

He said, "So never be afraid
To do jobs, big or small,

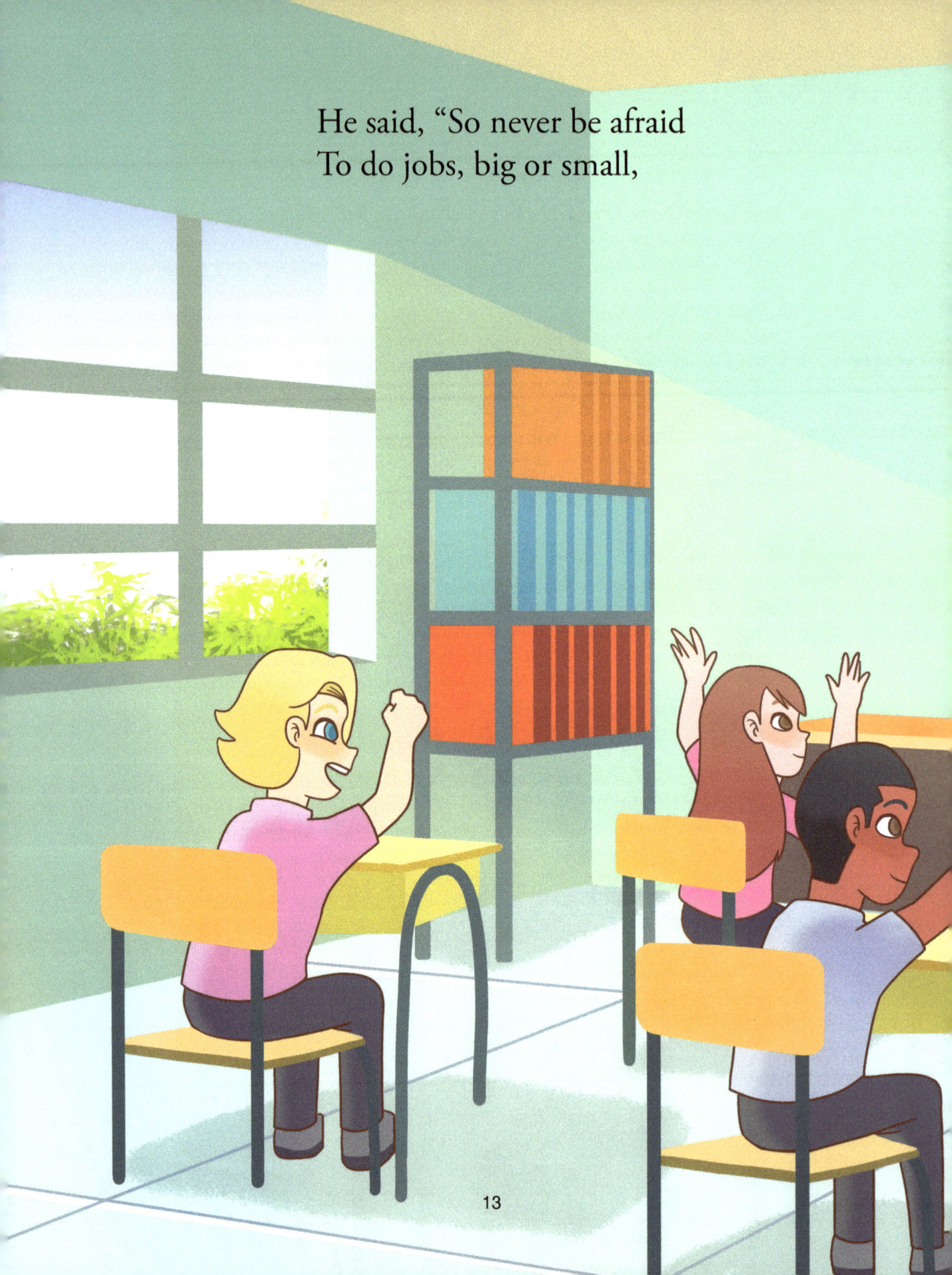

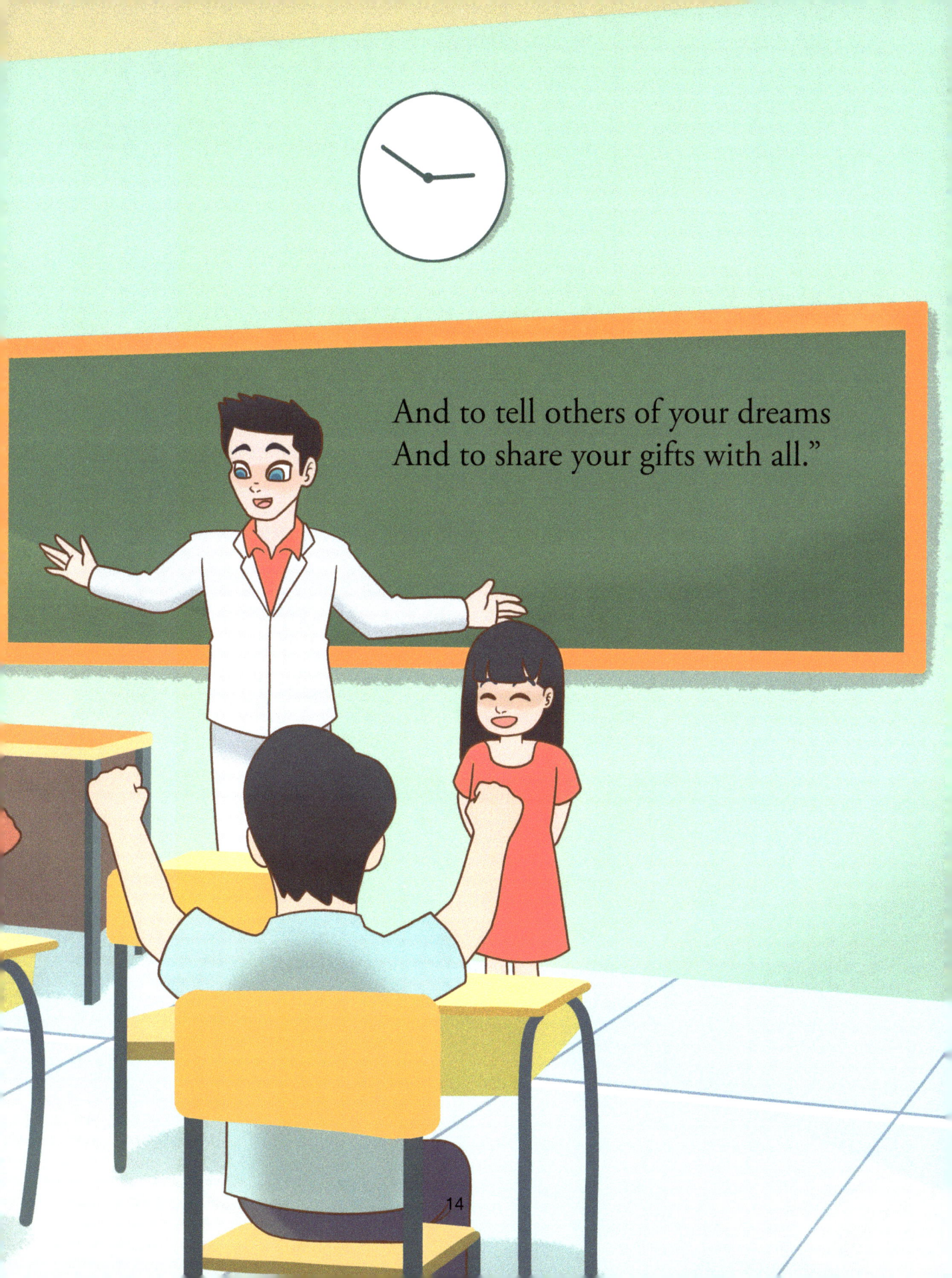

And to tell others of your dreams
And to share your gifts with all."

I was so happy to know we are safe,
To talk about our dreams at school.

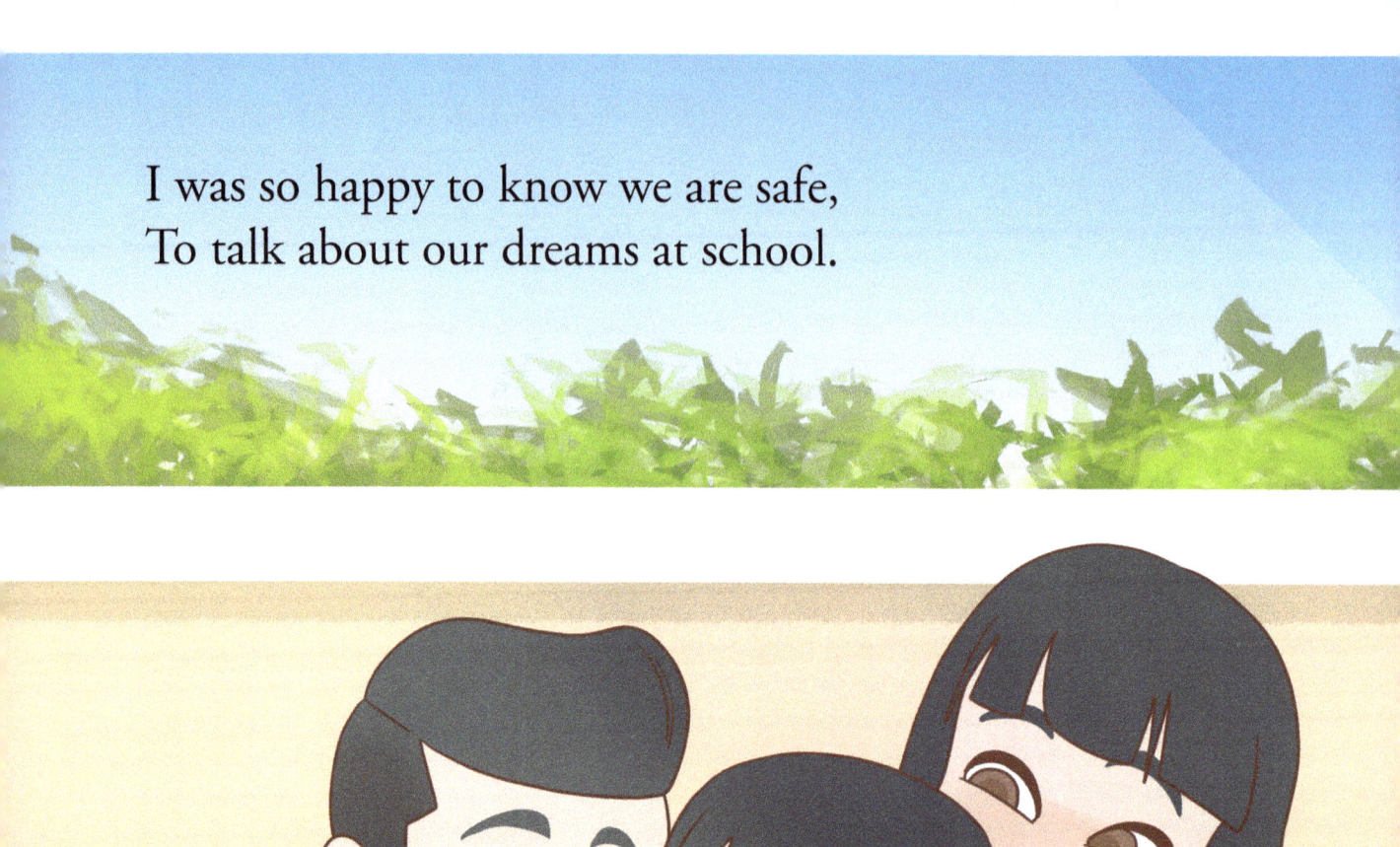

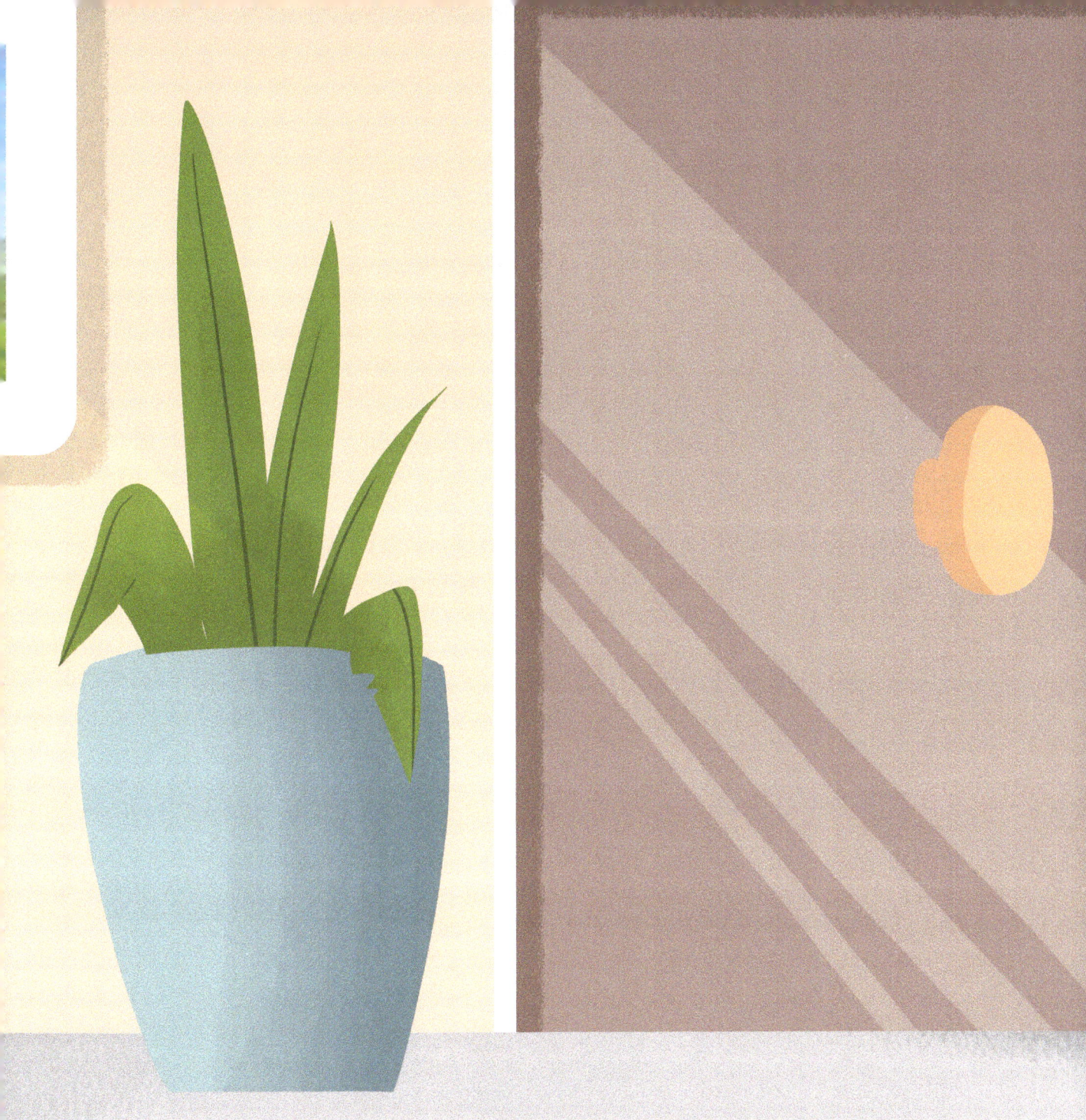

And *no matter* what we do when we grow up,
We can make a better world for me and you!

About the Author

Stacy Price, PhD, has been an educator for twenty years. She has a passion for writing about acceptance and is proud to unveil this series of children's books to highlight the focus on kindness and love for children just learning to read for the first time. She is a Pennsylvania native and is a proud mother of five children herself. She also enjoys hiking, her two dogs, and time with her family and friends.